Table of Contents for April • May

Table of Contents for June

Introduction

April • May • June—Instant Ideas for Elementary Teachers is filled with wonderful spring activities for your classroom. Ideas are ready-to-use and will make your classroom a fun place to learn.

Note! There are three more Instant Idea books we have written for you that contain many exciting monthly activities. These books will help brighten every day in your classroom—all year long!

FS-8311 *September • October*
FS-8312 *November • December*
FS-8313 *January • February • March*

Barbara Gruber   Sue Gruber

April Ideas

Welcome April!

Have each student make a colorful poster for the month showing the April flower (sweet pea) or gemstone (diamond).

April Bulletin Board

Focus on fairy tales during the month of April. Hans Christian Andersen was born on April 2, 1805, in Denmark. Gather a few fairy tale books by Andersen and others to read to your class. Then turn your classroom into a fairy tale festival with this bulletin board.

Ideas for Captions:

- Fairy Tale Festival
- The Land of Fairy Tales
- Fairy Tale Magic
- The World of Fairy Tales

1. Cover the bulletin board with colorful paper. Add a caption.
2. Have students select a favorite fairy tale. Reproduce the castle pattern on page 8 for each student. Students color and cut out the fairy tale castle. Then they write the title of their favorite fairy tale on the castle.
3. Have students paste lined paper on the back of the castle and write a summary of the fairy tale. Younger students can simply write a sentence about the fairy tale below the title.

Castle Pattern

Teacher: Use with "Fairy Tale Festival" idea explained on page 7.

April Vocabulary Ideas

April

1. showers
2. flowers
3. rain
4. umbrella
5. tulip
6. daffodil
7. spring
8. birds
9. robin
10. nest
11. rabbit
12. bunny
13. egg
14. basket
15. fools
16. day
17. joke
18. trick
19. lamb
20. chicks
21. lily

Instant Vocabulary Book

Take a few minutes to create an Instant Vocabulary Book to use all year long. Fasten ten 9" x 12" pieces of tagboard with rings as shown. Label each page with a month of the school year. Write and number seasonal or monthly vocabulary words on each page. As you think of additional words, add them to the appropriate page. Keep this handy book on the chalk ledge as an instant reference for yourself and your students.

Use the word lists to give instant assignments that require no preparation. For example, assign students to write the even numbered words in alphabetical order.

rab bit

See pages 10, 29, 30, 49 and 50 for more vocabulary activities.

Scrambled Eggs

Have each student cut 10 "eggs" from pastel construction paper. Students print a word on each egg. Then they cut through the egg and the word to create two halves as shown. Next they scramble the egg halves and exchange them with a partner. Students paste the matching halves on paper.

Word Puzzles

Reproduce the graph paper on page 10. Have students make word shape puzzles for 10 vocabulary words from the instant vocabulary book. Remind students not to number the words or put them in the same order as in the vocabulary book. Students exchange papers and fill in the word puzzles.

egg

April Word Hunt

Reproduce the word hunt worksheet on page 10. Students can use the April words to make a word hunt. Then they exchange papers and solve the word hunt created by a classmate.

Name ______________________________ Skill: Vocabulary

Vocabulary Word Hunt

1. Write 10 vocabulary words on the lines.
2. Write those 10 words on the puzzle grid. Be sure to write some words across and some down.
3. After writing the vocabulary words on the grid, fill in the blank spaces with letters.

Teacher: Use with vocabulary activities on page 9.

Spring Writing Activities

The S P R I N G Writing Booklet

This Spring Writing Booklet can be used any time during April, May or June. Reproduce page 12 for each student. Have students color and cut out the letters. Give each student a seven-page construction paper booklet. Pages can be any size (6" x 9" works well). Students paste the title on the cover and a letter on each page as shown.

Writing activities for each letter:

Spring makes me think about...

Practice makes perfect. Use your best handwriting to copy this sentence: April showers bring beautiful May flowers.

Rain makes plants and flowers grow. Write a haiku poem about spring flowers. Haiku pattern: Lines #1 and #3 have five syllables, line #2 has seven syllables.

In the spring, the weather gets warm. Make a list of 10 things you like to do outdoors in spring.

Now is the time for birds to build their nests. Draw pictures showing birds building a nest, caring for eggs, and feeding baby birds in the nest.

Gardens are planted in the spring. Make a colorful picture of a vegetable or flower garden. Write a sentence about your picture.

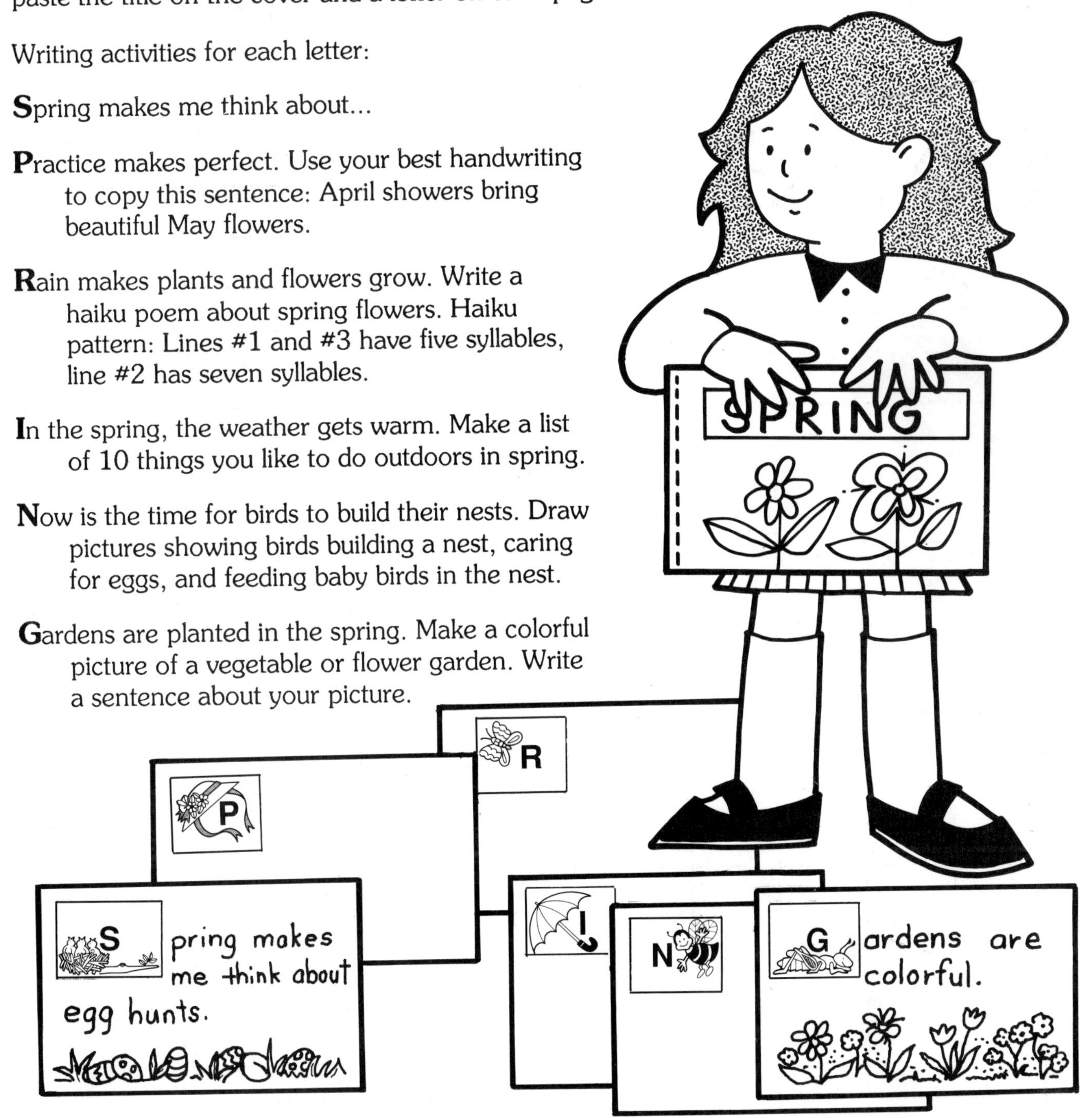

Helpful Hint! Work on the Spring Writing Booklet over a period of time. Collect and store the booklets after each assignment so they don't get lost!

Spring Writing Booklet

Teacher: Use with "Spring Writing Activities" explained on page 11.

April Poetry Activities

Poetry Fun for April

Have students use the Clerihew poetry pattern to write a poem about themselves. Each line can have any number of words or syllables. To make the poems funny, have students exaggerate.

Clerihew Pattern

Line #1 ends with the person's name.
Line #2 rhymes with line #1.
Lines #3 and #4 rhyme with each other.

Energetic Annie Dunn,
Likes to have a lot of fun.
She really loves to sing and dance,
In bright green polka-dotted pants.

It's fun to play with Bobby Frye.
He really is quite a guy.
You should see him up at bat.
No one else can swing like that!

2-4-6-8 Animal Poems

Pets-Are-Wonderful Month is celebrated in April.
Have students write a 2–4–6–8 poem about a pet.

Line #1 has two words.
Line #2 has four words.
Line #3 has six words.
Line #4 has eight words.

My cat
Puff is so fluffy,
Her soft fur is all gray.
She curls up on my bed at night.

Spring is a good time to concentrate on pet care. See pages 17–18 for more ideas to highlight pet ownership.

April Science Activities

Thomas Jefferson, the third president of the United States, was born on April 13, 1743. A talented gardener, he was one of the first people in America to eat tomatoes rather than grow them for mere decoration. Tomatoes did not become a popular food until after the Civil War.

Encourage your students to become indoor gardeners with these activities.

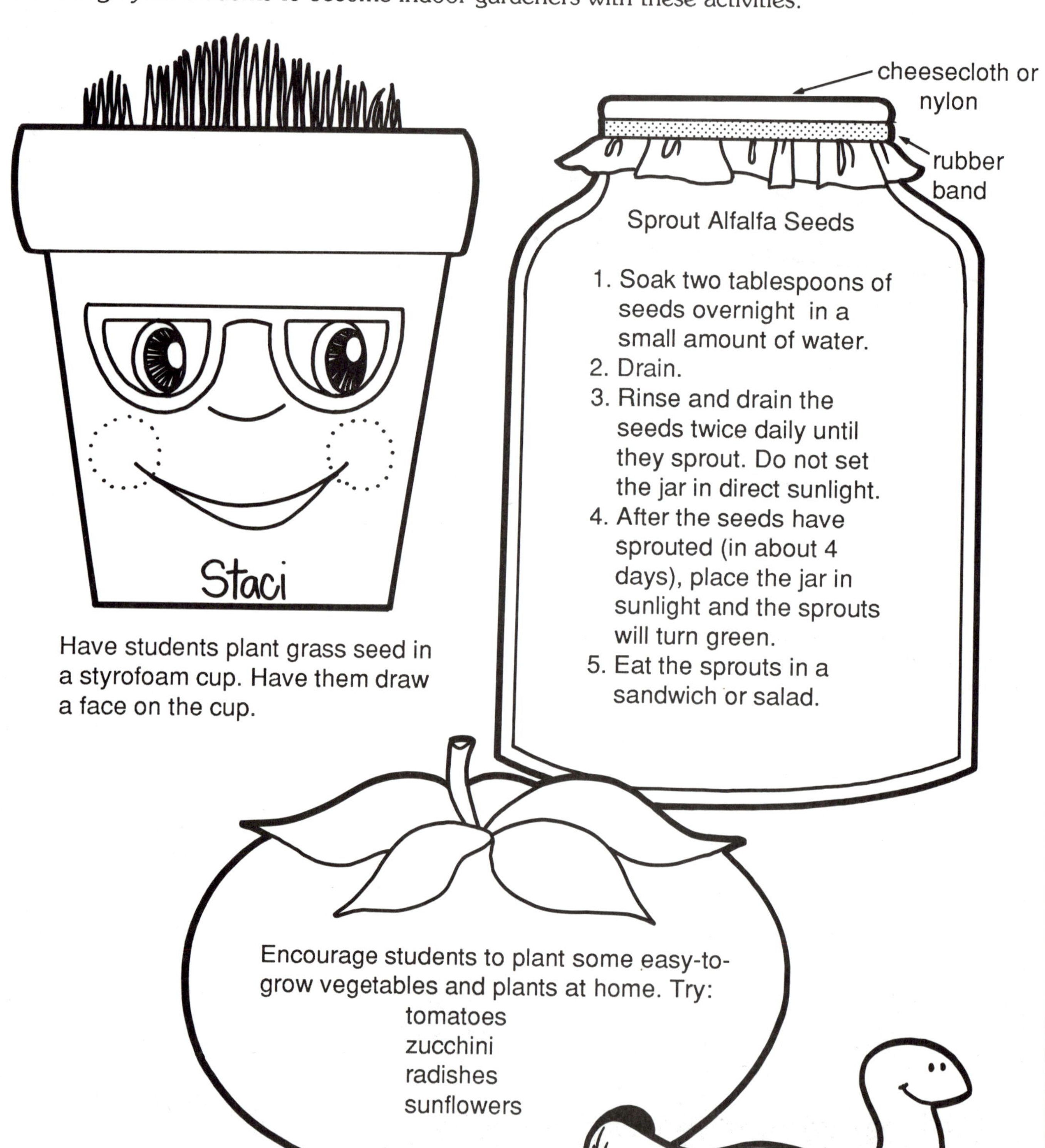

Have students plant grass seed in a styrofoam cup. Have them draw a face on the cup.

Sprout Alfalfa Seeds

1. Soak two tablespoons of seeds overnight in a small amount of water.
2. Drain.
3. Rinse and drain the seeds twice daily until they sprout. Do not set the jar in direct sunlight.
4. After the seeds have sprouted (in about 4 days), place the jar in sunlight and the sprouts will turn green.
5. Eat the sprouts in a sandwich or salad.

Encourage students to plant some easy-to-grow vegetables and plants at home. Try:

tomatoes
zucchini
radishes
sunflowers

More ideas on page 15.

April Science Activities

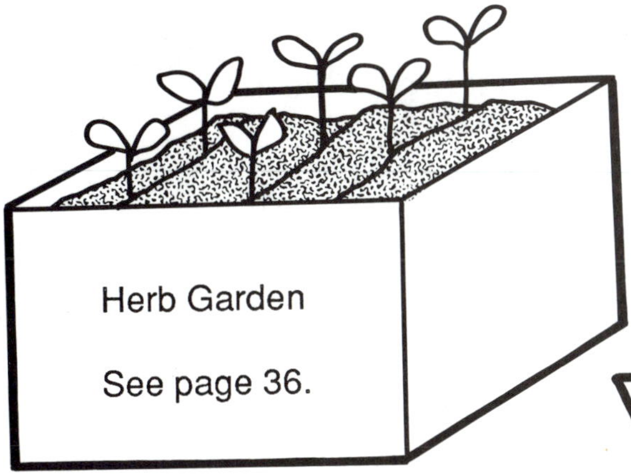

Herb Garden

See page 36.

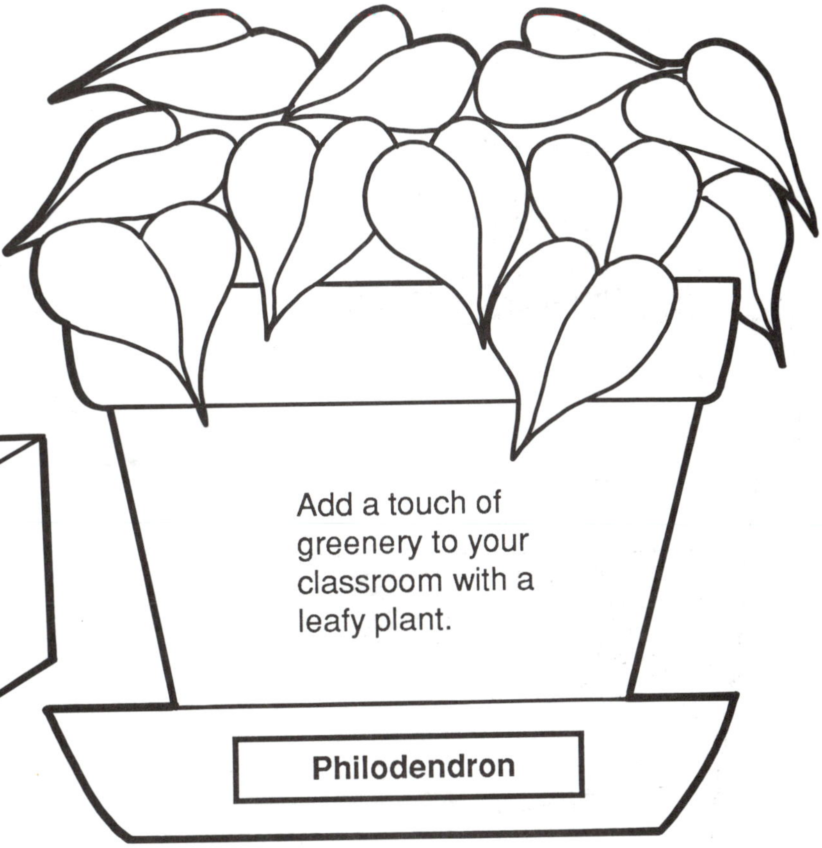

Add a touch of greenery to your classroom with a leafy plant.

Philodendron

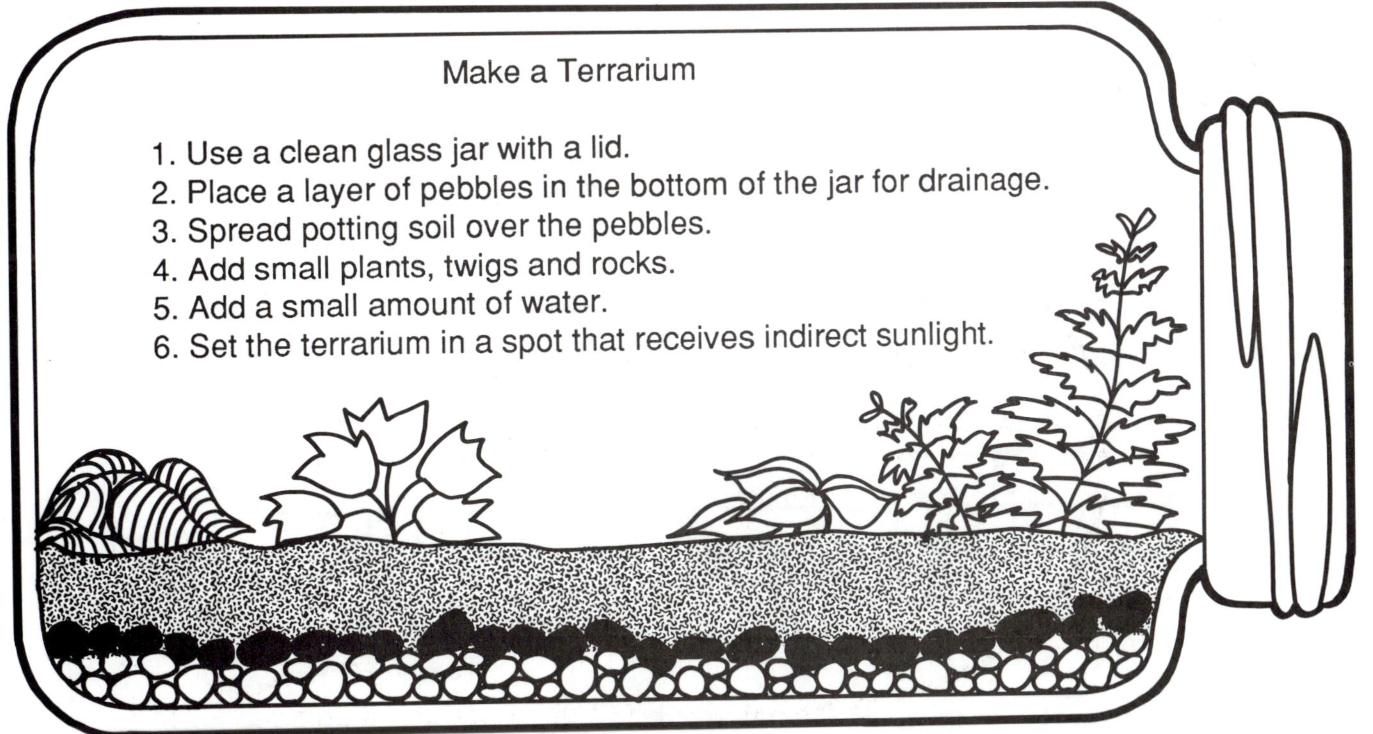

April Holidays and Special Days

Pets-Are-Wonderful Month is celebrated in April! Focus on the world of pets with these high-interest activities.

Pets Have Rights

Have a class discussion on caring for different kinds of pets. Record ideas from your class to create a Bill of Rights for pets entitled *Pets Have Rights.* Write the final Bill of Rights for pets on butcher paper.

Pets Have Rights

• Pets have the right to be fed.
• Pets have a right to a safe place to sleep.

A Wonderful Pet

Have students write sentences describing a wonderful pet. Be sure they tell what makes the pet wonderful. Then, have students draw a picture of the pet.

A Graph About Our Pets

Make a bar graph to show the kinds of pets owned by your students.

Our Pets

dog
cat
gerbil
fish
bird

April Holidays and Special Days

A Day in the Life

Have students draw a time line showing an ideal day in the life of a pet.

A Report About a Pet

Have students write a pet report. You may ask students to do individual reports on a pet they have or would like to have, or have students without pets team up with those that do to prepare a report together.

Have students include this information in the report:

- a description of the pet
- where it sleeps
- what it eats
- how it came to be the family pet
- cute things the pet does
- other interesting facts about the pet

MY PET REPORT by Derrick P.

Finally, have students make a cover for the report with a colorful illustration of the pet.

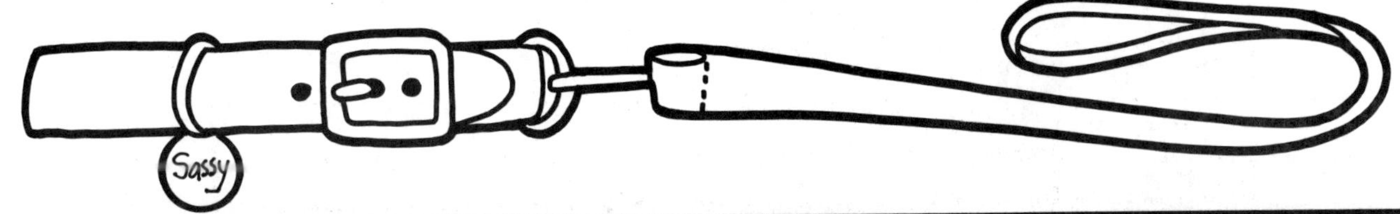

April Holidays and Special Days

Ho Ho, Hee Hee Humor Month

April is National Humor Month. Have a jolly time in your classroom making a joke book! Provide an assortment of joke, limerick and riddle books from the school library for students to use. Have each student copy and illustrate a favorite joke or riddle. Staple them into a booklet for your classroom library.

The Not-So-Itsy-Bitsy Spider—An April Fools' Day Play

Your students will enjoy presenting this amusing play about an April Fools' Day prank! To add to the fun, put on the play for another class.

Reproduce the play on pages 19 and 20.

Name ____ Skill: Reading a play

The Not-So-Itsy-Bitsy Spider

(A Play for April Fools' Day)

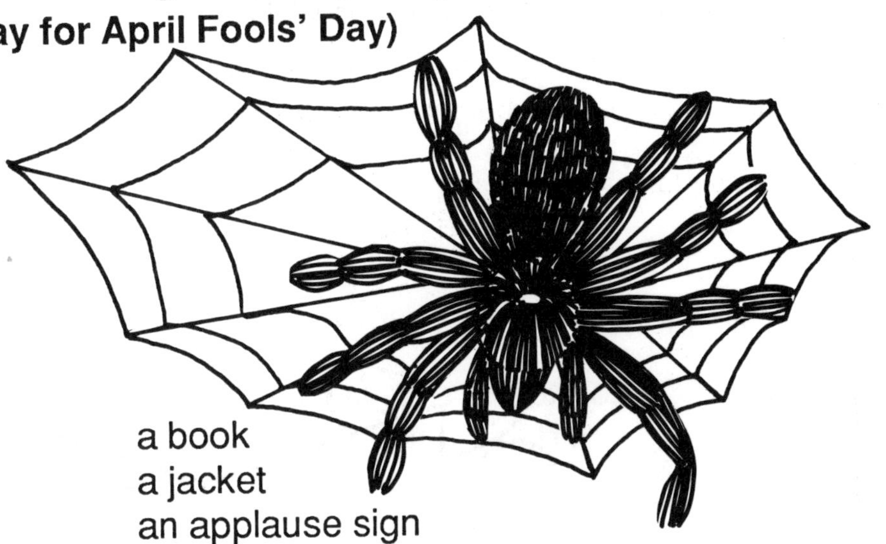

Characters:

Andrea Brown *a girl*
Mrs. Brown *Andrea's mother*
Mr. Figbee *a neighbor*
Announcer *a boy*

Props:

a black spider *made from paper*
a cage *box or bag*
two chairs, placed side by side
a book
a jacket
an applause sign

Announcer: We are proud to present *The Not-So-Itsy-Bitsy Spider*. We hope you enjoy our play.

(Mrs. Brown is seated, reading a book. Andrea is looking for her pet spider.)

Andrea: Oh no...Mr. Fuzzy, my pet spider, is not in his cage. Where can he be hiding? I'd better tell Mother about this!

(Announcer knocks on table like someone knocking on a door.)

Mrs. Brown: Andrea, please answer the door. It's Mr. Figbee, our neighbor. His birthday is today, April first, so I invited him over.

(Andrea opens the door. Mr. Figbee is at the door.)

Andrea: Hello, Mr. Figbee. Please come in.

(Mr. Figbee enters and sits beside Mrs. Brown. He puts his jacket on his lap.)

Mr. Figbee: My goodness, your Andrea is getting so big!

(Andrea rolls her eyes.)

Andrea: Excuse me, Mother and Mr. Figbee. I've been searching everywhere for Mr. Fuzzy. Let me know if you see him. Oh, by the way, Mr. Figbee, Mr. Fuzzy is a big black tarantula.

(Mr. Figbee looks startled, wiggles a bit, and picks up his feet.)

Teacher: The conclusion of the play appears on page 20.

Name ______________________________ Skill: Reading a play

The Not-So-Itsy-Bitsy Spider (continued)

Mrs. Brown: Andrea, you've scared Mr. Figbee.

(Andrea continues looking for her spider. Meanwhile the announcer places the spider on Mr. Figbee's jacket so the audience doesn't notice.)

Andrea: Where can he be? I hope no one steps on him!

(She continues looking for the spider.)

Andrea: Look! There he is *(pointing at the jacket)*. Sit perfectly still, Mr. Figbee, and don't make a sound. I'll get Mr. Fuzzy.

Mrs. Brown: (*sighing*) Oh dear!

Mr. Figbee: Andrea, you silly girl. I **know** what day this is. I'll just pick up this toy spider and pop it into my jacket pocket. *(He picks up the spider and puts it into his pocket.)* There...no more spiders.

Andrea: But Mr. Figbee, that spider **isn't** a toy. It is a real live tarantula. Please give Mr. Fuzzy back to me so I can return him to his cage.

Mr. Figbee: Oh Andrea, you're not fooling me for one minute. Don't you think I know it's April Fools' Day? Okay, here is your spider *(handing spider to Andrea)*.

Mrs. Brown: Now Andrea, enough about spiders. Put Mr. Fuzzy away this minute.

Andrea: Mr. Fuzzy, you look hungry. Let's get you something to eat.

Mrs. Brown: (*sternly*) Andrea...

(Andrea shrugs her shoulders and walks away talking to Mr. Fuzzy.)

Andrea: Well Mr. Fuzzy, it seems **you** were the one who played an April Fools' Day trick on Mr. Figbee. He thought you were only a toy, not a real live tarantula!

Announcer: We hope you have enjoyed our play *(holds up applause sign)*.

Teacher: The play begins on page 19.

April Holidays and Special Days

Celebrate books in April! April 2nd is International Children's Book Day and the birthday of Hans Christian Andersen. (See the "Fairy Tale Festival" bulletin board idea on pages 7 and 8.) Also in April is National Library Week, celebrated the third full week of the month. Have students do these follow-up activities after they read a story or book.

- Write a different ending for the story.
- Give a short oral book report.
- Write sentences about what happened at the beginning, middle and end of the story.
- Design a new cover for the book.
- Make a sequence of three pictures about the story.
- Make a bookmark.
- Read your favorite part aloud.
- Write about your favorite part of the story.
- Act out an exciting part of the story with a partner.

April Holidays and Special Days

Stitch a Scene

Read a chapter a day from a book to your class. Tell students that they will be making a stitchery of their favorite part of the book. After you have finished reading the book, give each student a rectangle of burlap for the stitchery.

Ask parents to donate yarn.

Use light-colored burlap such as yellow, beige or blue.

Ask a parent helper to run a line of machine stitching around the edge of the burlap as shown. This prevents fraying and allows students to fringe the border. Or, put masking tape around edges to prevent fraying.

A straightened paper clip can be used as a yarn needle.

Teach a few students how to do a particular stitch (running stitch, back stitch, cross stitch...). List students' names on the chalkboard as "stitchery teachers."

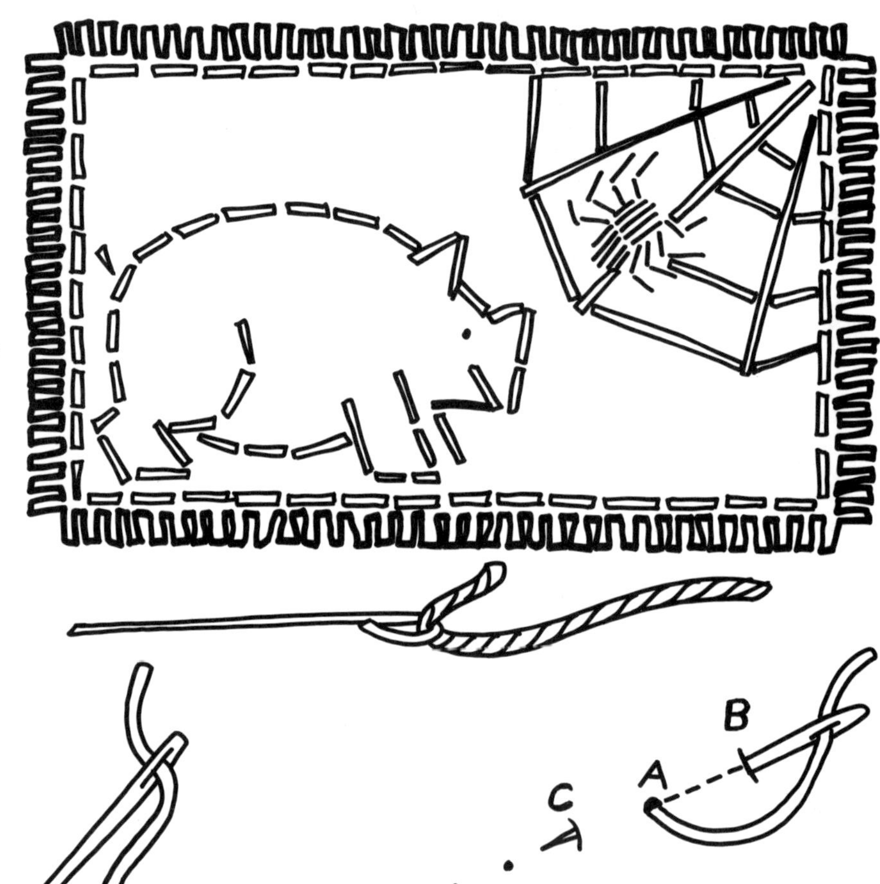

RUNNING STITCH

BACK STITCH

Bevy of Bunnies Garland

Trace or reproduce the bunny pattern on page 23. Have each student make one bunny. Encourage students to use paper scraps to decorate the bunnies with hats, baskets and clothing. Make a bunny garland by pasting together the paws as shown. Display the Bevy of Bunnies Garland on a bulletin board, wall, or along the windows in your classroom.

Bunny Pattern

Teacher: Use with "Bevy of Bunnies Garland" idea explained on page 22.

April Holidays and Special Days

John James Audubon, a famous American naturalist, was born on April 26, 1785. He used watercolors to make realistic paintings of birds.

Audubon Art

Your students can learn about birds by making colorful bird illustrations. Gather books about birds for your students to use. Have each student select the bird he wants to draw and sketch it lightly in pencil. Then, students use watercolors or crayons to color their drawings. Have students label the birds.

Ideas for Displaying Audubon Artwork:

Make a paper quilt as shown. After displaying the quilt in your classroom, hang it in the school office, library or cafeteria for others to enjoy.

Display artwork on a bulletin board.

Staple pictures into a booklet about birds. Add the booklet to your classroom library.

April Holidays and Special Days

April Enrichment Activities

Use this list of enrichment activities in a variety of ways. Select an activity for a class assignment or list the activities on the chalkboard as extra credit work.

Activities for students:

1. Hans Christian Andersen was born on April 2, 1805. Read one of his fairy tales. Make a roll movie.
2. The first Arbor Day was celebrated in Nebraska on April 10, 1872. Now Arbor Day is celebrated on different days in different places. It is a day set aside for planting trees. Collect a leaf from three different kinds of trees. Identify the kinds of trees the leaves are from.
3. Beverly Cleary has written many books for children about Ramona and Henry. Her birthday is April 12. Read a book by this author. Make a bookmark about one of her books.
4. Daylight Savings Time begins the first Sunday in April at 2:00 A.M. Make a sign to remind family members to set the clocks ahead on the right day. Remember, it's spring forward, fall back.
5. National Coin Week is celebrated the third week in April. Make a coin bank from a box, can or jar to use for saving coins. Figure out how much money you would have if you saved:

   three pennies every day for one year *($10.95; $10.98 leap year)*
   one nickel every day for one year *($18.25; $18.30 leap year)*
   one dime every day for one year *($36.50; $36.60 leap year)*

6. Make a Happy Easter or Welcome Spring greeting card. Give the card to someone special.

More Ideas for April

See pages 60, 62, 63 and 64 for a reproducible open skills worksheet, a parent newsletter and handy note paper.

May Ideas

Welcome May!

Have each student make a colorful poster for the month showing the May flower (lily of the valley) or gemstone (emerald).

May Bulletin Board

May baskets filled with flowers will add a touch of springtime to your classroom.

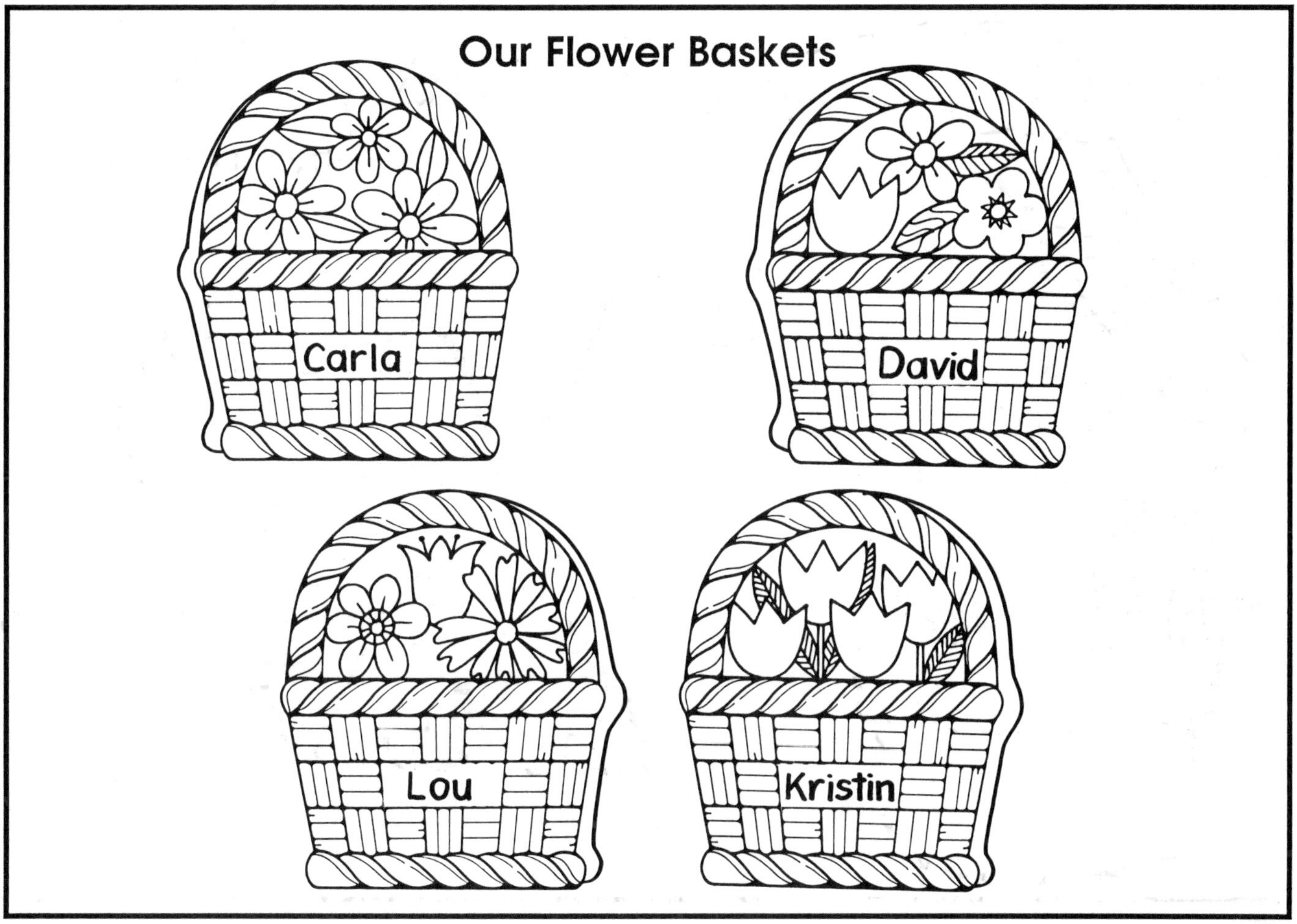

Our Flower Baskets

Carla David

Lou Kristin

Ideas for Captions:

- Our Flower Baskets
- A Tisket, a Tasket
- Baskets of Blossoms
- Spring Flowers

Directions:

1. Cover the bulletin board with colored paper. Add a caption.
2. Have students cut out the basket pattern from page 28 and trace it two times on pastel construction paper, or make several tagboard basket patterns for students to trace.
3. Students paste the two baskets together leaving the center of the basket open to insert flowers.
4. Have students use paper scraps to make flowers, leaves and stems for their baskets.

Flower Basket Pattern

Teacher: Use with the May Bulletin Board idea explained on page 27.

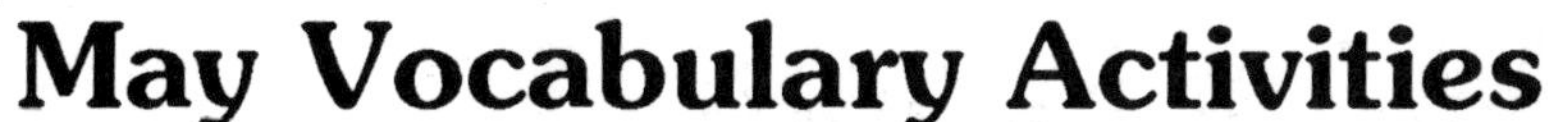

May Vocabulary Activities

Instant Vocabulary Book

Add the May words to your Instant Vocabulary Book (see page 9). Use the vocabulary activities on pages 9, 10, 30, 31, 49 and 50.

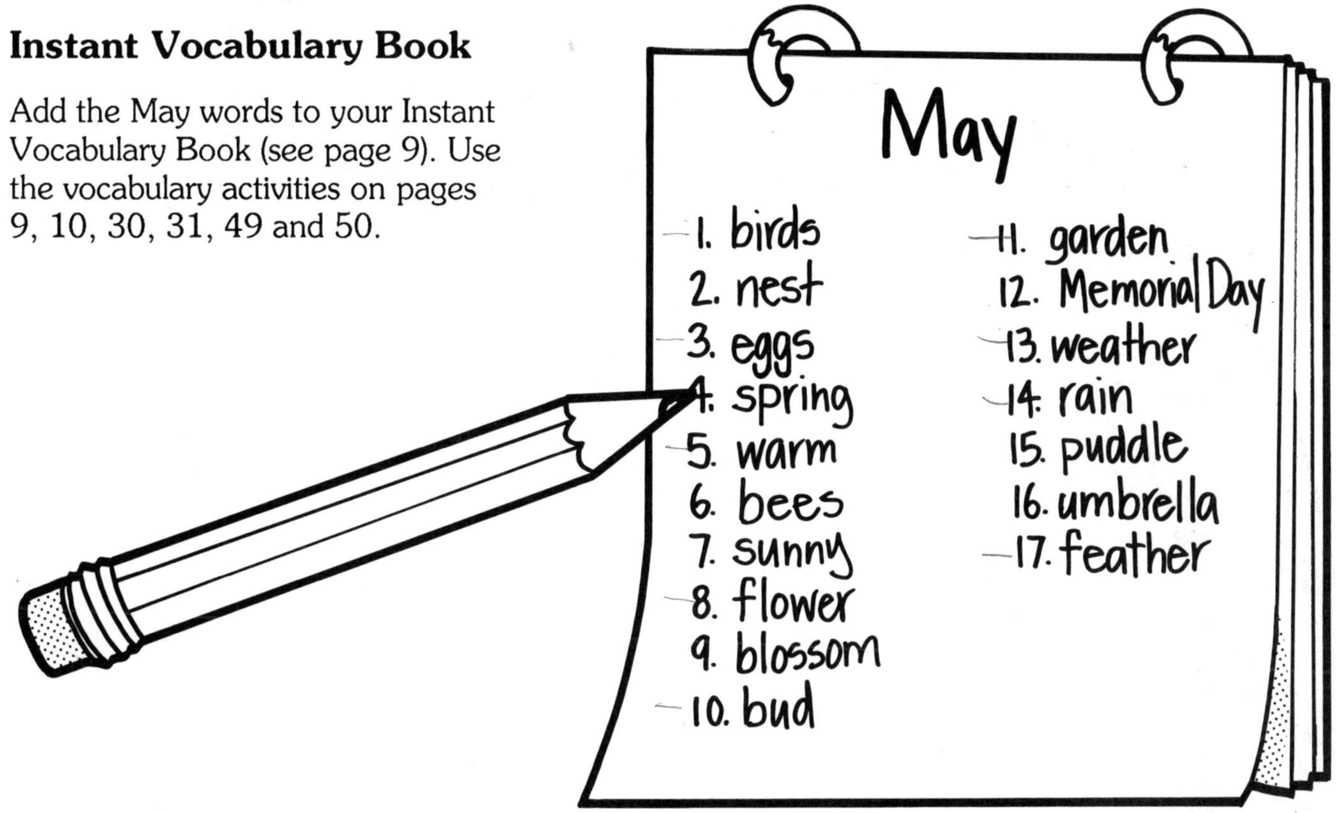

May
1. birds
2. nest
3. eggs
4. spring
5. warm
6. bees
7. sunny
8. flower
9. blossom
10. bud
11. garden
12. Memorial Day
13. weather
14. rain
15. puddle
16. umbrella
17. feather

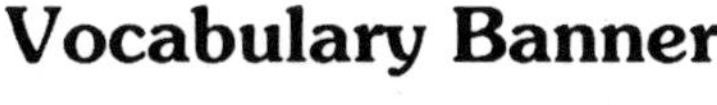

Vocabulary Banner

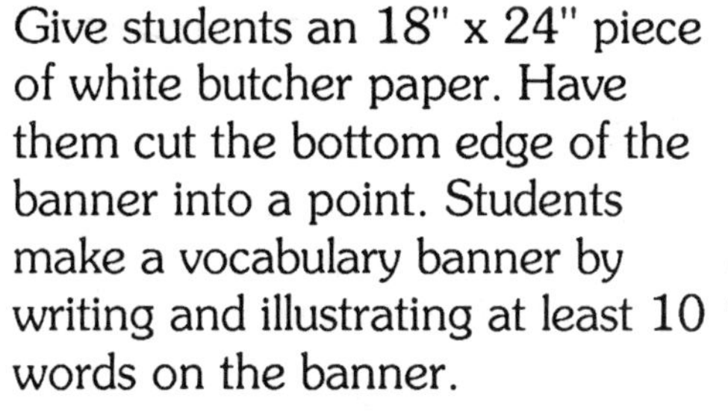

Give students an 18" x 24" piece of white butcher paper. Have them cut the bottom edge of the banner into a point. Students make a vocabulary banner by writing and illustrating at least 10 words on the banner.

Attach the banner to a wire hanger by folding over the corners and stapling.

Billy
flower
sunny
eggs
nest

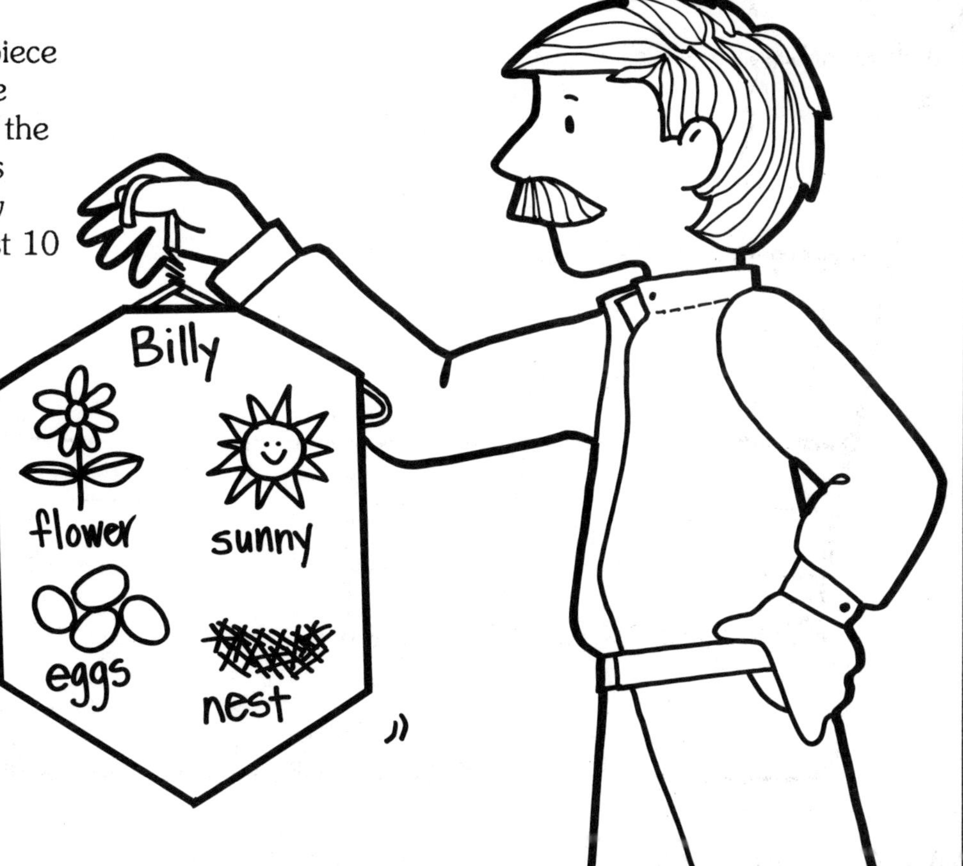

May Vocabulary Activities

Grow Little "Grow Worm"

Have students cut 10 ovals from light-colored construction paper. Tell them to write a May vocabulary word on each oval. Then students arrange the words in ABC order and paste them together to make a "grow worm." Have students add a face, legs and antennae as shown.

Can You Remember?

Hold up the vocabulary book (or write a list of words on the chalkboard). Have students look at the words for one minute. Then, put the words away and have students write as many as they can remember.

Rhyme Time

Have students write as many rhyming words as they can for the May vocabulary words.

May Poetry Activities

Time for Tanka Poetry

Spring is the time when trees and flowers to begin to grow. Have students write a tanka poem to welcome spring.

Tanka is an unrhymed form of poetry consisting of five lines.
Lines #1 and #3 have five syllables each.
Lines #2, #4, and #5 have seven syllables each.

Teach your class how to write this form of poetry by writing on the chalkboard your own poem or this example:

The great oak stands tall—
Green and brown, silent giant
Dropping small acorns
To the ground so far below.
His children will soon be trees.

Ask for ideas from your student to compose a class poem in tanka form.

Mother's Day Poems

Cinquain (sing KĀN) poems make wonderful verses for Mother's Day cards. Have each student create a cinquain about his mother.

Cinquain Pattern

Line #1 one word (usually the title)
Line #2 two words (describing line #1)
Line #3 three words (describing action)
Line #4 four words (a feeling)
Line #5 one word (synonym for line #1)

Mother
busy, smiling
likes to jog
makes me feel happy
Mom

May Science Activities

Be-Kind-to-Animals Week is celebrated the first full week of May. Try these interesting science activities about the world of animals.

Picture This!

Animals with backbones are called vertebrates. Have students fold their papers into six sections. Label the sections as shown. Have students draw and label an example of these types of vertebrates.

Who's Who?

Write these categories on the chalkboard:

Pets Farm Animals Wild Animals

Ask students to name different animals. Discuss the category to which each animal belongs. List the animals on the chalkboard under the right headings.

Be Kind to Birds

Make a bird feeder as a treat for the birds in your area.

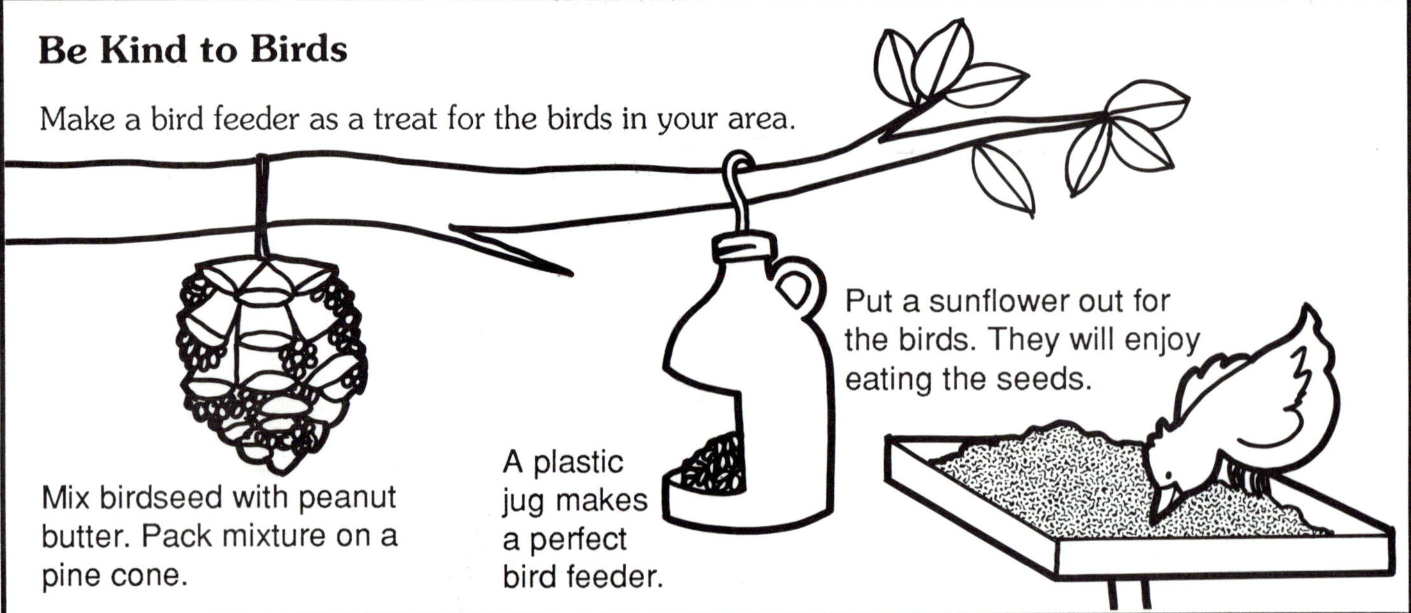

Mix birdseed with peanut butter. Pack mixture on a pine cone.

A plastic jug makes a perfect bird feeder.

Put a sunflower out for the birds. They will enjoy eating the seeds.

May Holidays and Special Days

Signs of Spring

Spring festivals and Maypole dances are held at the beginning of May to celebrate spring. Use the spring shapes on page 35 to make templates. Students can trace the templates on construction paper for these spring activities. Shapes can be decorated with crayons, paper scraps, yarn or ribbon.

Plant Sticks

Add a decorative touch to a house plant with a plant stick. Use tape or glue to attach a paper shape to a plastic drinking straw or wooden craft stick. Use the shapes on page 35.

Students can add a plant stick to the flower basket bulletin board on page 27.

Signs-of-Spring Bookmarks

Attractive bookmarks can be made from a strip of colorful construction paper and one of the shapes on page 35!

Bookplates

Students can make a bookplate for one of their books decorated with a signs of spring shape from page 35.

May Holidays and Special Days

Springtime Streamer

Have students select several shapes to paste on a construction paper streamer. Use the shapes on page 35.

Springtime Mobiles

Spring shapes are perfect for mobiles! Glue two identical shapes back-to-back to hide the string.

Spring Art

Students choose one or two shapes and paste them on construction paper. They then incorporate the shapes into a springtime picture.

Signs-of-Spring Shapes

Teacher: Use with projects described on pages 33 and 34.

May Holidays and Special Days

Mother's Day is observed on the second Sunday in May. Help your students show appreciation to someone special with these ideas.

Windowsill Herb Garden

A miniature herb garden makes a wonderful gift for someone special. Put potting soil in styrofoam cups or foil mini-loaf pans. Plant seeds for easy-to-grow herbs such as parsley, sage or chives.

For a special touch, add a plant stick to each herb garden. Directions for plant sticks are on page 33.

Mother's Day Poetry

Give that special person a poem (see page 31).

Mother's Day Gift

The Father's Day note pad on page 57 can also be made for Mother's Day.

Greeting Cards for Special People

Have students create this clever three-part card. The pattern and directions are on page 37.

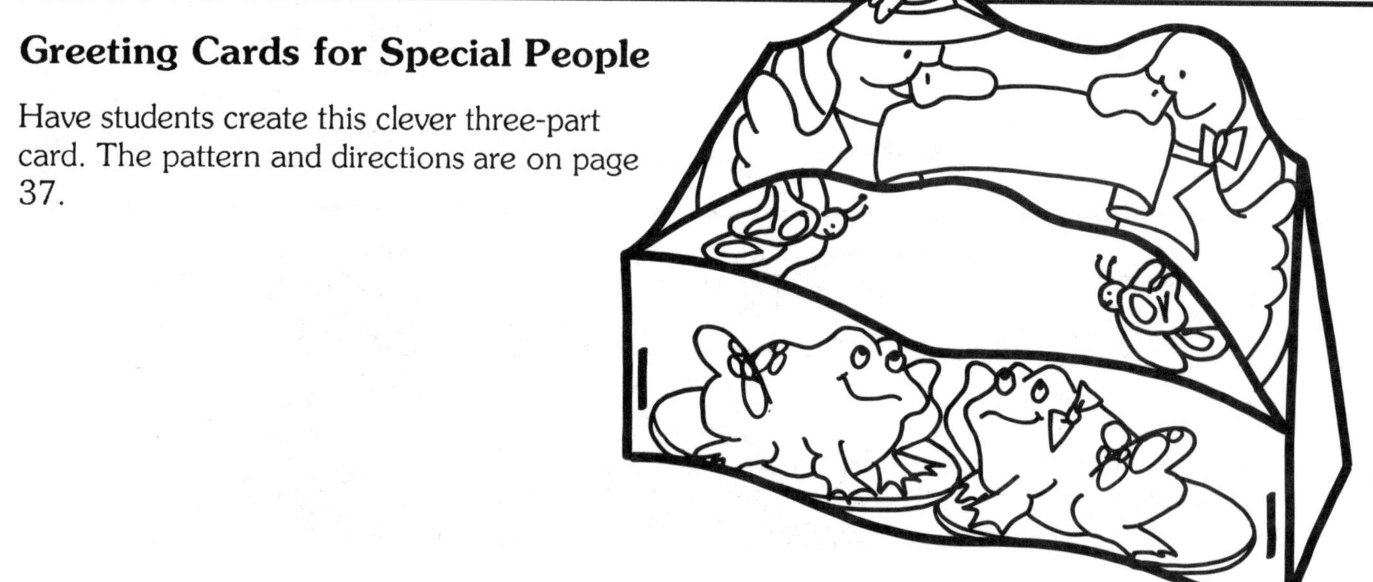

Greeting Card

Teacher: Use as a Mother's Day, Father's Day or thank-you card.

May Holidays and Special Days

National Music Week is celebrated the first full week of May.

World's Best Kazoo Band

Have your students practice singing a folk song or patriotic song that everyone knows. Then teach your class how to play the kazoo. Each student needs a comb and a piece of wax paper or plastic wrap. Wrap the comb in paper as shown. Have students hum the song with their lips parted to make the kazoo vibrate.

Perhaps your World's Best Kazoo Band can perform for another class!

The Golden Spike—A Play

On May 10, 1869, a railroad spike of solid gold was used to join the railroad tracks that ran from east to west. Now passengers and freight could travel coast to coast by rail. Teach your students about this important event in American history with the reproducible play *The Golden Spike* on pages 39 and 40.

Name ________________________________ Skill: Reading a play

The Golden Spike—A Play (Part 1)

This play is about the joining of railroad tracks from east to west in 1869.

Characters:

Announcer #1
Announcer #2
Reporter #1
Reporter #2
Reporter #3
Reporter #4
Reporter #5
Mr. Stanford, president of the Central Pacific Railroad
Mr. Durant, vice president of the Union Pacific Railroad

Props:

golden spike *made from yellow paper (about 7 inches long)*
hammer *ruler with foil or paper hammer head*

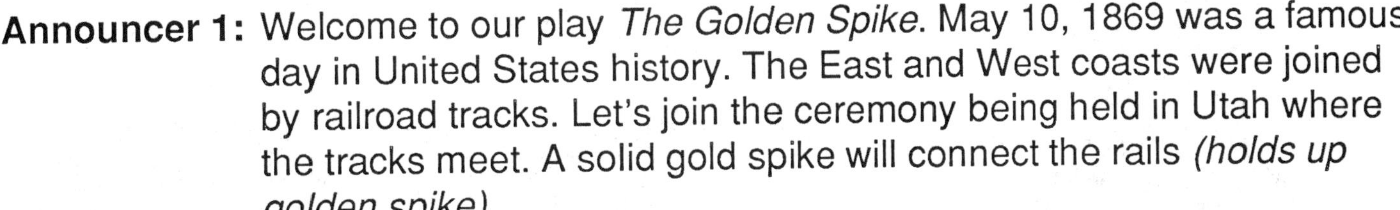

Announcer 1: Welcome to our play *The Golden Spike*. May 10, 1869 was a famous day in United States history. The East and West coasts were joined by railroad tracks. Let's join the ceremony being held in Utah where the tracks meet. A solid gold spike will connect the rails *(holds up golden spike).*

Announcer 2: The golden spike is cast from twenty-dollar gold pieces. It is engraved "The Last Spike." Mr. Stanford, president of the Central Pacific, and Mr. Durant, vice president of the Union Pacific, will take turns striking the gold spike. Mr. Stanford will go first *(hands hammer to Mr. Stanford).*

Reporter 1: A telegraph wire is attached to the spike. It will send a signal to the world the instant the spike is struck.

Reporter 2: In San Francisco, the fire bell in city hall will ring and a 200-gun salute will be fired.

Reporter 3: In Philadelphia, the Liberty Bell will ring.

Reporter 4: In New York, there will be a 100-gun salute and church bells will ring.

Reporter 5: Parades will be held in many cities.

Teacher: Part 2 of *The Golden Spike* appears on page 40.

Name ______________________________________

The Golden Spike—A Play (Part 2)

(Announcer 1 holds the golden spike in position to be hit.)

Mr. Stanford: Our railroad workers crossed mountains, fought snowstorms, and cut tunnels through solid rock to bring the railroad here. Many men died working on the railroad. As president of the Central Pacific Railroad, I will strike the blow that will be heard around the world.

(Mr. Stanford swings and misses the spike. Reporters look surprised. Mr. Stanford hands the spike to Mr. Durant.)

Mr. Durant: Thank you. Many of our men also gave their lives for the railroad. Our workers crossed rivers and deserts. They fought fierce battles with Indians to bring the railroad here. As vice president of the Union Pacific Railroad, it is an honor to join the rails.

(Durant swings and misses on purpose. Stanford and Durant shake hands and everyone cheers.)

Announcer 1: Others were then invited to tap the golden spike in place. It was then removed to be put on display in a museum.

Announcer 2: America was no longer cut in two—the East and West were joined by the railroad.

Announcer 1: People moved from the east to the west. Farms and towns grew. Thanks to the railroad our country grew stronger and richer.

Announcer 2: May 10, 1869 was an important day for America. We hope you enjoyed our play.

Teacher: Part 1 of *The Golden Spike* appears on page 39.

May Holidays and Special Days

Springtime Safety

Spring and summer days mean more outdoor activities for everyone. Spring is a good time of the year to focus on safety.

Emphasize recreational safety while camping, hiking, swimming and boating. It is also important to focus on transportation safety such as pedestrian, bicycle and car safety. These activities will help your students learn important safety rules.

Bumper Stickers

Make safety bumper stickers with strips of construction paper or tagboard.

Signs for Safety

Use construction paper to make signs featuring important safety rules. Each sign should have a colorful illustration and a safety rule or slogan.

May Holidays and Special Days

Safety Certificate Award

Reproduce the It's-Smart-to-Be-Safe certificate on page 44. Paste the certificate on construction paper. Award it to students upon completion of a unit on safety.

I Pledge to Be Safe

Reproduce the Safety Pledge on page 44. Have each student choose an area in which he feels he needs to be more aware of safety rules. Each student fills out a Safety Pledge.

Safety Badge

Reproduce the badge on page 44. Paste it on construction paper. Have each student write a safety rule or slogan on the badge. Declare a "Safety Badge Day" on which all students wear badges during the school day.

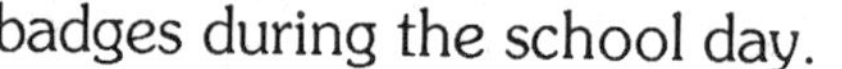

May Holidays and Special Days

It's-Smart-to-Be-Safe Booklet

Use white construction paper to make a four-page booklet for each student. Pages should be approximately 6" x 9" and stapled together on the left. Have students draw and cut out an oval slightly larger than a quarter on the first page of the booklet as shown. Next they trace the cut-out oval onto page two, and cut out that oval (which will be in the same position on that page). They do the same for page three. On page four of the booklet, they draw the oval but do not cut it out.

Each student draws and colors his face in the oval on page four. Then students draw themselves being safe in their home. On the other three pages, they draw themselves being safe on a bicycle, in a car, and around water. The face drawn on the last page of the booklet shows through the oval cut-out on each page.

Students add a construction paper cover and paste the It's-Smart-to-Be-Safe certificate (on reproducible page 44) on the front of the booklet.

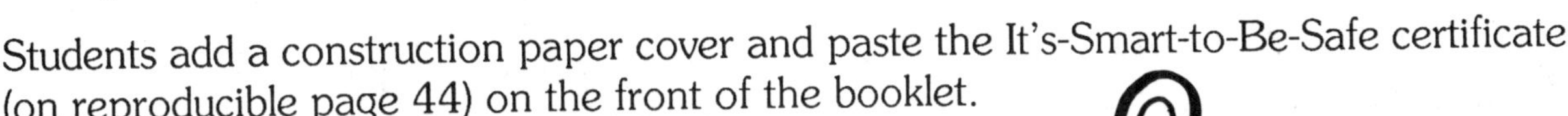

1. Staple four pages together.

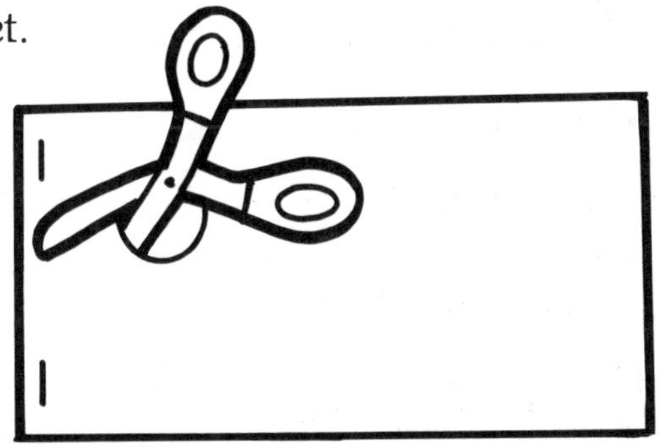

2. Draw and cut out an oval on page 1.

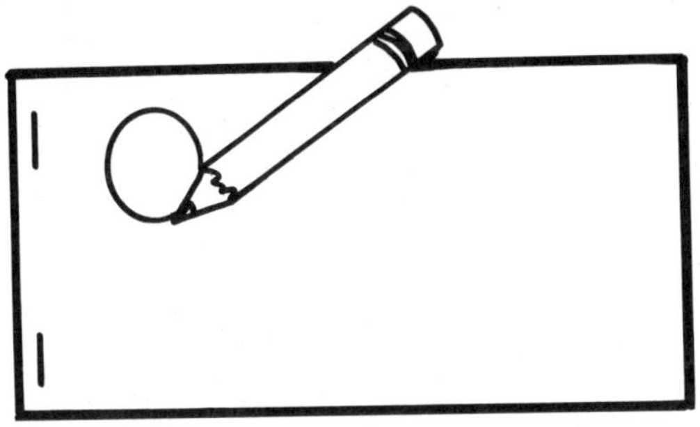

3. Trace the opening on page 1 onto page 2.

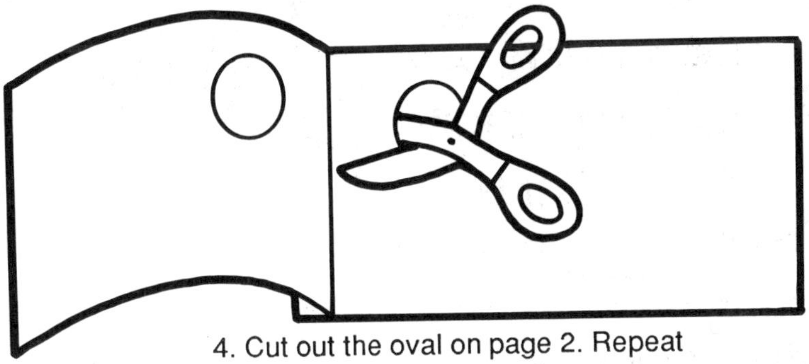

4. Cut out the oval on page 2. Repeat steps 3 and 4 on page 3.

5. On page 4 trace the oval but do not cut it out. Instead draw your face.

I use a mitt.

6. The face will show through for you to draw the four action scenes.

Name ______________________________ Skill: Learning about safety

It's Smart to Be Safe!

At school we learned about ______________

____

____

____

Student ________________________________

Teacher________________________________

School ________________________________

Safety Pledge

I pledge to obey the safety rules

when I ______________________________

____

____

Name ________________________________

Date ________________________________

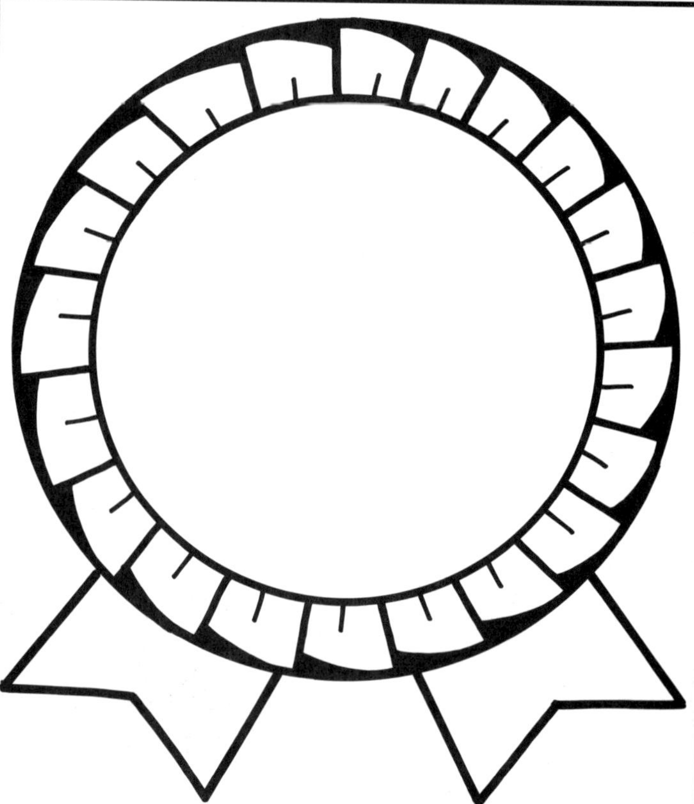

1. Write a safety rule on the badge.
2. Draw a picture.
3. Color and cut out the badge.
4. Wear the badge.

Teacher: Use with safety awareness ideas on pages 41–43.

May Holidays and Special Days

May Enrichment Activities

Use this list of activities in a variety of ways. Select an activity for a class assignment or list the activities on the chalkboard as extra credit.

Activities for students:

1. Be-Kind-To-Animals Week is celebrated the first full week in May. Do something kind for your pet or someone else's pet. Draw a picture showing what you did.
2. Aviation history was made in the month of May. Look up information about Charles Lindbergh or Amelia Earhart. Draw a picture of one of these famous aviators and tell why he or she is important to aviation history.
3. In England, in 1840, the first adhesive postage stamp was issued. Save canceled postage stamps from mail that comes to your house during the month of May. How many different stamps did you save? Bring the stamps to school at the end of the month.
4. National Transportation Week is in May (the week including the third Friday). Make a flag showing six different kinds of transportation. Mount it on a stick or rolled-up paper mast.
5. May has 31 days. Make up five math problems that have *31* as the answer.
6. Memorial Day honors people who have died, especially in the service of their country. Make an American flag to hang in your window.

More Ideas for May

See pages 60, 62, 63 and 64 for a reproducible open skills worksheet, a parent newsletter and handy note paper.

June Ideas

Welcome June!

Have each student make a colorful poster for the month showing the June flower (rose) or gemstone (pearl).

June Bulletin Board

Welcome sunny summer days with this June bulletin board. Add to the fun by putting up a countdown of numbers to show the days remaining until the beginning of summer vacation.

Ideas for Captions:

- Summer Splashdown
- Sunny Summer Days
- In the Good Old Summertime...
- Splash Into Summer

Directions:

1. Cover the bulletin board with yellow or white paper. Add a caption and a bright yellow or orange sun. Add blue paper to represent water as shown.
2. Reproduce page 48 for each student and have each student make the figure look like himself or herself in a swimsuit. Tell students to draw their own likeness on the swimmer by adding facial features and hair. Next have them write on the inner tube how it might feel to bob around in the water in an inner tube. Finally have students color and cut out the swimmers and mount them on the bulletin board.

Swimmer Pattern

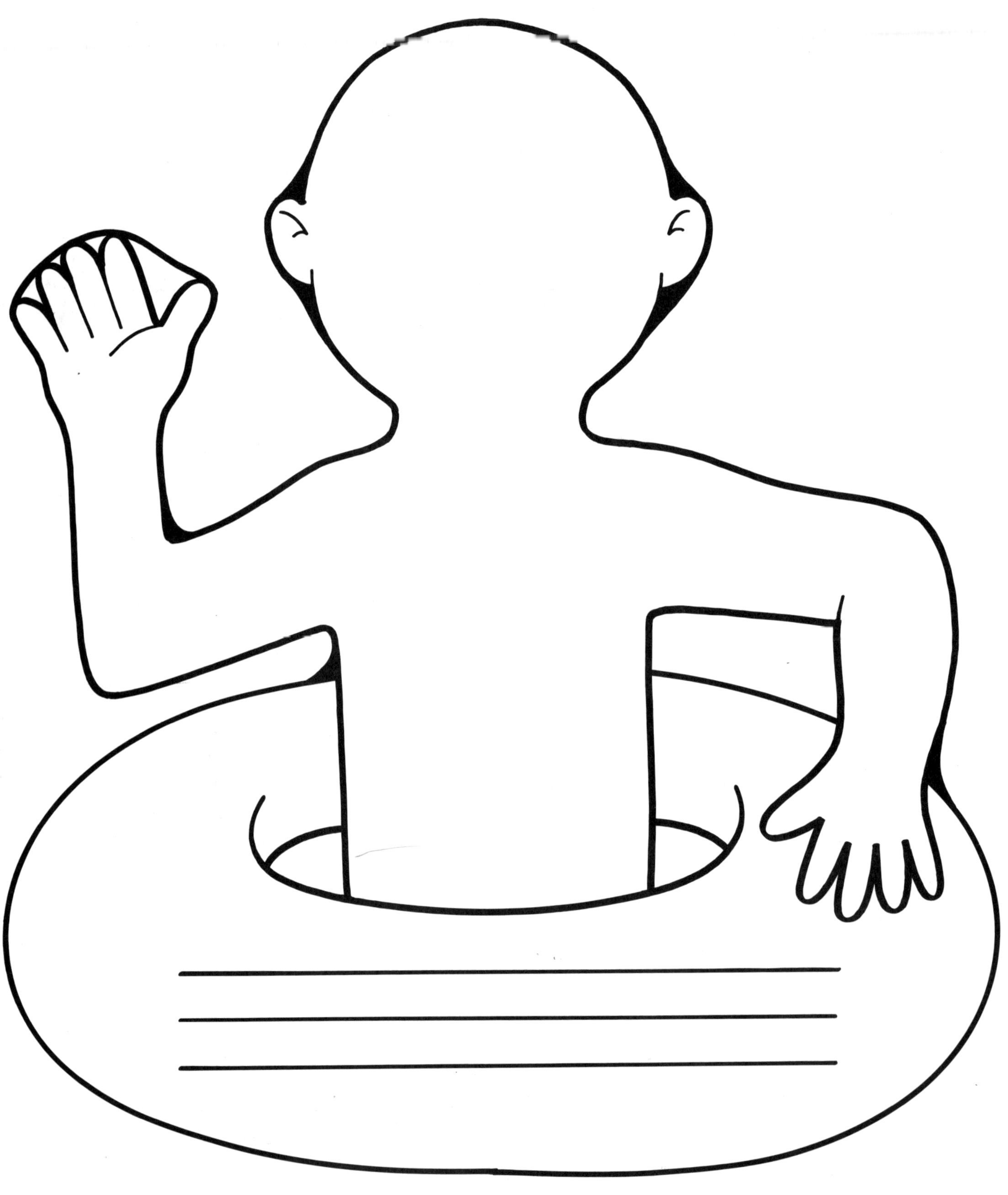

Teacher: Use with "Splashing Into Summer" idea explained on page 47.

June Vocabulary Activities

Instant Vocabulary Book

Add the June vocabulary words to your Instant Vocabulary Book (see page 9). Use the June word list with the vocabulary activities on this page and on pages 9, 10, 29, 30, 50 and 51.

1. summer	11. play	21. travel
2. July	12. beach	22. party
3. August	13. sun	23. sunburn
4. vacation	14. bicycle	24. lake
5. school	15. picnic	25. hot
6. camp	16. trees	
7. trip	17. grass	
8. suitcase	18. garden	
9. swim	19. vegetables	
10. fish	20. flowers	

Story Time

Write a story using at least 10 of the June vocabulary words. Underline the 10 words with a yellow crayon.

What's Missing?

Have students write 10 vocabulary words leaving out the vowels. Students exchange papers and fill in the missing letters.

Vocabulary Bingo

Reproduce the bingo grid on page 50. Have students print 24 words from the vocabulary list, one word per square. Call out words on the vocabulary list to play bingo.

Name ______________________________ Skill: Vocabulary

Vocabulary Bingo

Teacher: Use with "Vocabulary Bingo" described on page 49.

June Poetry Activities

Poems As Easy As 1-2-3

As a prewriting activity, discuss with students their favorite summer activities. List on the chalkboard some descriptive words mentioned by students. Then suggest the following easy-to-write poetry patterns to let your students become instant poets. As the titles suggest, the only restriction is the number of words in each line.

1-2-3 Pattern

Example: swimming
diving board
watch me jump

1-2-3-2-1 Pattern

picnic
good food
games to play
fun friends
ants

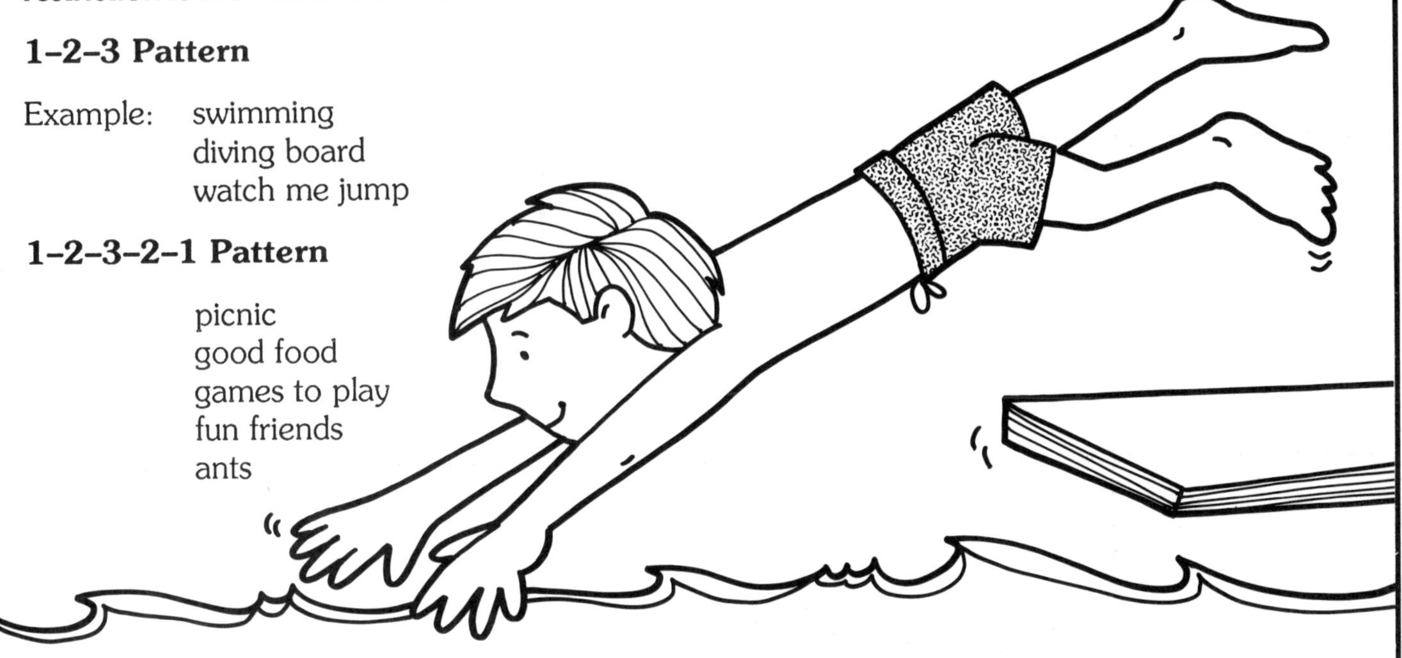

A Scoop of Summer

Summer vacation is just around the corner. Have students use the reproducible worksheet on page 52 to write words about summer. Then they can use those words to write a poem about summer. For extra fun, have students copy their summer poem on a paper "scoop" of ice cream. Add a brown paper cone and post on a bulletin board for a "yummy" poetry display.

Name ______________________________ Skill: Writing a poem

Summer Poetry

Write words that make you think of summer.

Summer Words

______________ ______________
______________ ______________
______________ ______________
______________ ______________
______________ ______________
______________ ______________

Use your summer words to write a poem.

____

____
____
____
____
____
____
____

Teacher: Use with "A Scoop of Summer" described on page 51.

June Science Activities

World Environment Day, June 5, is a day to focus on ways to preserve and enhance our environment. Increase students' awareness of the world around them with these activities.

Give Our World a Helping Hand

Have a class discussion about things we can do to help make our world a cleaner place to live. Have each student trace a handprint on green construction paper and cut it out. On the handprint have students write an idea for improving the environment. Arrange the handprints on a "tree" cut from brown construction paper.

One, Two, Three Pickup!

Have each student decorate a grocery bag to use as a litter bag! Have students write an anti-litter slogan on it!

The Playground Cleanup!

Take your class to the playground to pick up litter for five minutes. Have each student bring a litter bag. Invite another class to join you in this activity. After the playground cleanup, make sure students wash their hands. Then, have both classes play an outdoor game together!

Mention the playground cleanup to your school principal. Perhaps your students will receive recognition for enhancing the school environment.

June Holidays and Special Days

Teacher Thank-You Week is the first week of June. With these activities students will learn to express appreciation by giving teachers a well-deserved pat on the back.

Teacher Thank-You Greeting Card

Have students choose a person at the school who has helped them—perhaps the librarian, a former teacher, an instructional aide, or the speech pathologist. Each student makes a card of appreciation for that person. Use the greeting card idea on pages 36 and 37.

Teacher Awards

Perfect Pencil Award

Have students use yellow construction paper to make a large pencil and pink construction paper for the eraser. Each student writes a message and presents the pencil to a favorite teacher.

To:

Thank you for

From:

To:

From:

Thank you for

An Apple for the Teacher

Have students use red and green construction paper to make an appreciation apple for a special teacher.

Thanks a Bunch!

Help your class say a big thank-you to someone special at school. Give each student a small white paper plate. Have him draw his face and write his name on the back of the plate. Paste the plates in the shape of a bunch of grapes on bright colored butcher paper. Add a stem and leaves and a few words of appreciation. Present the Thanks-a-Bunch banner to the school nurse, librarian, music, art or physical education teacher.

Wrap-Up-The-Year Activities

Perk up the last weeks of school with these high-interest activities.

Story Theater

Divide the class into four groups. Let each group act out a scene from a favorite story for the class. Choose one student to be the director for each group.

Autograph Poster

On the last day of school, have students make a poster* to collect autographs from school friends!

Ashley Green's
Autographs

John Hernandez
Kim Soo
Kelly Li
Angela Rye
Mark Way

*Use 12" x 18" construction paper.

Play a Game!

Play "I'm packing my suitcase and I'm taking..." The first student completes the sentence with the name of something beginning with *a,* such as *apple*. The next student repeats the first student's sentence and adds a word beginning with *b*. Play continues with each student adding an item beginning with the next letter of the alphabet. If a student forgets an item, the next person starts the game again with the letter added last.

A Note of Appreciation

Have each student write a note of appreciation to someone* at school. Have primary students dictate their notes to an older student.

*custodian
librarian
principal
cafeteria staff member

More end-of-the-year activities appear on page 56.

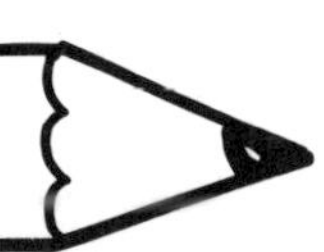

Wrap-Up-The-Year Activities

Here are more activities to perk up the last few weeks of school.

I Remember When...

Have students reflect on the school year. Each student selects a fond memory or special moment. Students write and draw a picture about it.

Summer Fun Books

Have students make a summer fun book. Students draw or write about things they want to do over the summer.

- books to read
- vacation plans
- special activities

June

July

August

Word Whiz Game

Reproduce or have students copy this grid.

	colors	animals	states
S			
U			
M		monkey	
M			
E			
R	red		
V			
A			Alaska
C			
A			
T			
I			
O			
N			

Set a timer for 15 minutes. On your signal students fill in as many words as possible. (Try this game with teams, too!)

Title Charades

Write titles of books and stories familiar to your class on cards. Divide the class into two teams. Teams take turns guessing the titles charade-style. A team earns a point if the word is guessed in one minute.

Teach your students these hand signals commonly used in charades:

two syllables

small word

long word

sounds like

June Holidays and Special Days

America-Is-Beautiful Post Card

National Flag Week is observed each year the week including June 14, Flag Day. Have students display their pride in the United States by designing a giant post card to celebrate a beautiful place in America. Reproduce page 58. Have students paste the post card format on a piece of white construction paper. Next have them imagine they are visiting a famous place in America. It might be a monument, a park, or a city. On the blank side of the paper, students draw a colorful picture of the place they are "visiting" using books or encyclopedias as references. On the other side, they address the post card and write a message to a friend or relative. Hang the post cards from a piece of yarn strung across your room as a patriotic tribute to America during flag week.

Washington Monument
Dear Jerry,
We visited the Washington Monument in Washington, D.C. It is very tall. We climbed to the top. We could see the whole city.
See you in a few days. your friend,
Marsha

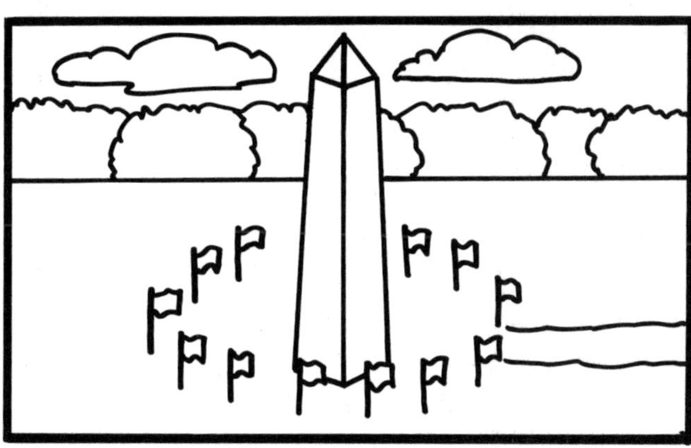

Father's Day Note Pad

Father's Day is celebrated the third Sunday in June. Have students make a fingerprint note pad as a Father's Day gift. Staple together six pieces of paper (white or light-colored) to make a note pad. Let students use a stamp pad to make a fingerprint on each page. Students use a fine-tipped pen to change each fingerprint into a different design.

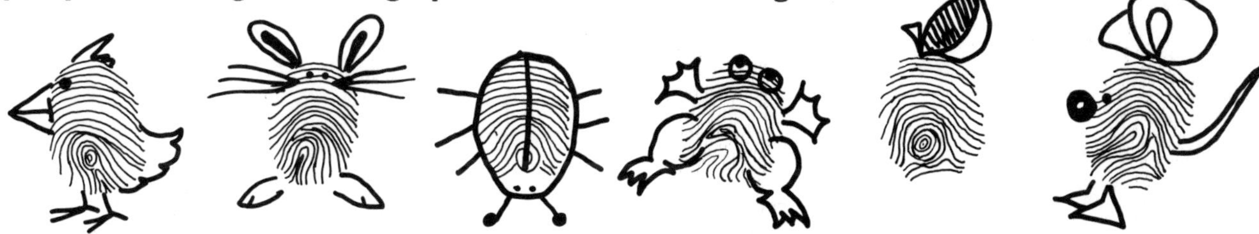

Father's Day Poetry

Have each student compose a poem to give Dad on his special day. See pages 31 and 51.

Father's Day Greeting Cards

See pages 36 and 37 for a greeting card idea that can be tailored to please any dad.

Name ______________________ Skill: Writing a post card

America-Is-Beautiful Post Card

Teacher: Use with “America-Is-Beautiful Post Card” idea explained on page 57.

June Holidays and Special Days

Flag Day is celebrated June 14. Americans feel patriotic when they see the United States flag. Inspire your students with these patriotic activities.

Patriotic Song Fest

Enjoy a song fest with your class. Declare a Patriotic Sing-Along Week and sing a different song each day. Many of your students may already know these favorite patriotic songs:

America
The Star-Spangled Banner
Yankee Doodle
You're a Grand Old Flag
America the Beautiful

Perhaps your music teacher will help with the celebration by giving students extra practice in learning and singing the songs, accompanying your group on the piano or guitar, or lending your students some instruments to perk up their performance.

If your school does not have a music teacher to enhance your patriotic sing-along, borrow recordings to help "strike up the band" as you sing!

The Pledge of Allegiance

Have your students copy the pledge of allegiance in their best handwriting and make a patriotic red, white and blue border around their paper.

I pledge allegiance...

My Flag

The colors and symbols on the United States flag have special meaning. Red stands for courage, blue for justice, and white for purity. The thirteen stripes stand for the original thirteen colonies. Each star stands for a state.

Have each student design a flag about himself on a piece of construction paper. The flag is to represent the person designing it and must display symbols and colors which stand for his positive qualities. On the back of the flag, the student writes the meaning of the colors and symbols he chose.

More Ideas for April, May and June

Summer Learning Activities

Reproduce page 61 for each student to take home a few days before the end of school. Parents will appreciate having a list of enjoyable activities for children to do over the summer months.

Reproducible Open Worksheet

Add directions and a skill activity to the reproducible worksheet on page 62. For example, write a math problem that is appropriate for your grade level on each tulip.

Name ____________ Skill

Directions:

1. 2. 3. 4. 5. 6. 7. 8. 9. 10. 11. 12.

Teacher: Add your own skill, directions and activity before reproducing this page for students.

Frank Schaffer Publications, Inc. 62 a reproducible page FS-8314 April-May-June

Parent Newsletter

Use "Read All About It" on page 63 to write a newsletter for parents. Then reproduce it for each child to take home.

Instant Reproducible Notes

Reproduce page 64 for instant note paper to use for parents, students, and colleagues. Use instant notes as student awards, too.

Name ____________________ Skill: Mixed review

Summer Learning Activities

Color the scoop of ice cream when you do the activity.

Reading

- Read for fifteen minutes.
- Make a bookmark about your favorite book.
- Read a recipe. Cook something with an adult.

Writing

- Copy a sentence from a book in your best handwriting.
- Write a poem or story. Draw a picture about it.
- Write a note to someone.

Just for Fun

- Write the alphabet. Write a word for each letter.
- Play a game with someone.
- Make a picture about having fun this summer.

Math

- Set the table. Count the total number of knives, forks, and spoons.
- If you save 10 cents a day in July and August, how much money will you have?
- Look at a grocery ad. Add the cost of three items in the ad.

Teacher: Use with "Summer Learning Activities" idea explained on page 60.

Name ______________________________ Skill:

Directions:

Teacher: Add your own skill, directions and activity before reproducing this page for students.

Name ______________________________

Read All About It

Newsletter to parents from:

____

Date ______________

To: ____________________

From: ____________________

Teacher: Use as note paper or student awards.